The Little Green Book of

Ayatollah Khomeini

Translated From Persian by

Daniel Deleanu, MA, MLitt, PhD

LogoStar Press

Toronto

ISBN: 978-1-4583-5581-2

Printed and bound in the USA.

CONTENTS

1

Islam: A Revolutionary Religion

Islam is the religion of those who struggle for the spirit of truth and justice, of those who clamour for freedom and self-determination. It is the abode of those who learn how to fight against the oppression of imperialism.

*

Our sole cure is to dethrone these perverted and perverting systems of government, and to bring down the traitorous, tyrannical and dictatorial gangs of sick rulers. This is the sacred duty of all Islamists in all Islamic countries. This is the one and only way to victory for all Islamic revolutions.

*

Those who live according to the principles of Islam should not be hesitant, if they truly wish to reestablish the political balance of society, and force all rulers to comply with the laws and regulations of Islam, with an armed sacred war against profane governments.

*

Lacking the means to prevent heresy or fight perversion does not imply that one should remain silent. If they hit you in the head, voice disapproval! One who submits to oppression commits a greater sin than the oppressor. Fight, vociferate, oppose, yell! Spread the truth: Islamic justice is not what they say it is.

*

Sacred war means victory over the profane world. Such a noble war may be declared once an Islamic government – which should be worthy of this name – has been formed under the supervision of the Imam, at his indications. It will then be the sacred duty of every fit adult male to willfully fight in this glorious war, whose golden aim is to install the Koran and its sacred law as the sole governor of the earth, from one end to the other. Yet, the entire world should understand that the hegemony of Islam is utterly different from the victorious preeminence of other vanquishers. That is why the Islamic government must be installed under the guidance of the Imam in order to insure the integrity of this sacred war, which will distinguish itself amongst all other tyrannical and unjust wars, creating such a sense of morality and such a degree of civilization that only Islam can beget.

*

Who freed our country and our people from the shameful

shackles of Zoroastrianism, if not the glorious army of Islam?

*

There are people among us who are not preoccupied with creating an Islamic movement, but, instead, of making a peaceful and quiet pilgrimage to Mecca with their Islamic brothers. Yet, one must know that it was not like that in the time of the Prophet. The Friday prayers were an opportunity to bring people together and call them to arms. The man who goes to war straight from the mosque fears only one thing: the Almighty. Death, material needs and homelessness are insignificant to him. An army of such men is an army of heroes.

*

Islamic belief and justice demand that within Islam, anti-Islamic governments not be tolerated. The empowering of a lay government would be similar to resisting the advancement of Islamic civilization. Any profane form of government, no matter what shape it may take, is undoubtedly an atheistic system, the instrument of Satan. Consequently, it is our duty to block its way and to fight vehemently against its disastrous results. Such Satanic authority can only give birth to deceivability on earth, the greatest of sins which must be mercilessly fought and completely uprooted.

In order to achieve that goal, we have no other way but to bring down all governments that do not act according to pure

Islamic laws, and are thus perverted and perverting, and to overthrow the traitorous, awful, unjust and dictatorial administrations that shamelessly serve them. That is not only our duty in Iran, but it is also the sacred duty of all Islamists in the world, in all Islamic countries, to take the Islamic political revolution to its final victory.

2

Islam and Imperialism

The West is nothing else but a haven of tyrants. That is why mankind must crush these dictators with an iron hand if it wishes to preserve its composure. If Islam had ruled the West, we would not have tolerated this savage behaviour, which surpasses in barbarity even the cruelty of wild beasts.

*

At a time when the West was so primitive that we have no documented history of it, when its people were still savages, and when America was still a territory inhabited by semi-wild redskins, the peoples of the Persian and Roman empires were forced to dwell in the terrible abode of tyranny, oligarchy, discrimination and dictatorship, with no right to take part in their own government. It was then that Allah, through his Prophet, gave us the laws whose magnificent goal has marveled all mankind.

*

The big country of Islam, united and indivisible, was broken up by the colonial attitude and the tyrannical demeanour of the imperialists. The nation of Islam, united and indivisible, was broken into several nations. And when the Ottoman Empire fought for Islamic unity, it was violently opposed by a common front of Russian, English, Austrian and other imperialist superpowers, which divided it, and annexed their territories.

*

Western missionaries, putting into practice secret schemes cunningly designed centuries ago, have established religious schools within Islamic countries. We did not protest, and this is what followed: the missionaries crept into our cities and villages in order to turn our own children into Christians and heathens.

*

The Islamic movement was first and foremost harmed by the Jewish people, who have been responsible for all anti-Islamic defamations and conflicts in the modern world. Then we should blame even more vehemently those terrible messengers of Satan, the imperialists. Within the last three centuries or even more, they have assaulted every Islamic country, wishing to wipe out Islam for once and for all.

*

Ever since the Crusades, they have been aware of the fact that only Islam, with its principles and its beliefs, can put a stop to their interests. They sent missionaries to many Islamic cities, where they found conspirators within the universities and different media centres, and made their specialists in Eastern Studies useful tools for the expansion of Western imperialism, all this with the purpose of distorting the truthfulness of Islam.

*

Their disgraceful plan is to keep us in our backward condition, to conserve our miserable life standard, so that they can exploit at large the great abundance of our underground resources, of our land, and of our labour force. They want us to stay on the breadline, ever insolvent and troubled on a daily basis by the nagging problems of survival, our poor living in constant need, so that we shall never realize the magnificence of the laws of Islam, which comprise solutions to all these terrible problems. They have done all this so that they can sit comfortably in the luxury of their big mansions, living their superficial lives in an idiotic way.

*

The source of this corruption lies mainly in the pack that is in power, and in the family of a whimsical tyrant who rules the country. These are the leaders who create all kinds of filth, such as prostitution and drugs, and who devote the revenues of the mosque to building theatre halls!

*

Islam has neither kings nor crowned princes. If that is a flaw, then Islam must be a flawed religion!

*

What do you comprehend of the unity between social life and religious tenets? And, moreover, what is in fact the social life that we have mentioned? Is it those ferments of immorality called theatre halls, movies, dancing and music? Is it the promiscuity of the young men and women who expose their arms, chests and thighs in public? Is it the ridiculous wearing of a hat as the Westerners do, or the import of their drinking habits? We are absolutely sure that they have forced you to trade your innate ability to distinguish between good and evil for a couple of transistor radios and ridiculous Western hats. Your attention has been forced to draw on the bare women seen in the public transit system and in swimming pools. Put a stop to these shameful habits, and let the dawn of a new life break through!

*

All the world's governments rely on the sharpness of their bayonets. We are not aware of any monarchy or republic in the entire world today which bases its policy on justice and good sense. They all stay in power only through coercion.

*

The leaders of our nation have been so much under the influence of the West that they have set the standard time of their country according to that of Europe (Greenwich Mean Time). This is really nightmarish!

*

In the past century, during which Western medicine and surgery were introduced into Iran, our leaders forsook our time-honoured medicine, and instead cheered when a couple of novices went abroad to study this damned Western medicine. Now we realize that such illnesses as typhus, typhoid fever, and the like can be cured only through long-established therapies that Western allopathic medicine does not possess.

*

The clerics must concentrate only on religious duties which comply with monotheism, the imparting of divine principles, and the uplifting of the people's morals. The army must also be controlled by the clergy in order to be functional and effective.

*

We [the clerics] firmly declare that refusal to wear the veil opposes the divine laws established by Allah and the Prophet, and is a material and spiritual offence for the entire country. We clearly state that the ridiculous wearing of the Western hat bars our way to freedom, and is against the will of Allah. We declare that mixed schools are a barrier on the way to a sound life: they are a material and spiritual insult for the country, and against the principles established by Allah. We also declare that music gives birth to immorality, covetousness and promiscuity, and discourages bravery and generosity towards others. It is prohibited according to Koranic principles, and must not be taught in schools. Radio Tehran, by broadcasting Western, Eastern and Iranian music, plays a despicable role by introducing immorality and promiscuity into upright families.

*

Theologians and other members of the clergy are not allowed to run the seminaries established by the government. State interference in this field is always a pretext for the demolition of the foundations of Islam, at the order of the western imperialists. This takes place in all Islamic countries, with no exception.

*

Clerics who, wearing ecclesiastical array, cooperate in one way or another with such theological schools must be spurned by all genuine believers.

It is strictly forbidden to connect with them, to engage in collective prayer in their company, to use their services for the dismissal of one's wife, to pay lawful alms to them, to invite them to perform funeral rituals, or to listen to their homilies at official meetings organized by the government with the single purpose of having them preach untruthfulness and blasphemous anti-Islamic concepts.

*

When the imperialists, the traitorous and despotic leaders, the Jews, the Christians, and the atheists have all grouped together to garble the truthfulness of Islam and to misguide the Islamic peoples, it is more than ever our sacred duty to act responsibly and organize an informative campaign.

*

We see today that the Jews – may Allah strike them down! – have maneuvered the editions of the Koran published in their occupied territories. We have to voice disapproval, to make all people understand that these Jews are planning to destroy Islam, and to establish instead a universal Jewish order. And since they are a foxy and enterprising people, I do fear – may Allah always preserve us from it! – that sooner or later they may be successful in reaching this mischievous goal, that through the frailty of some amongst us we may one day find ourselves under Jewish occupation – may Allah forever protect us from it!

*

A handful of scholars in the field of Eastern Studies, agents paid by the Western imperialists, are working diligently on the alteration of the eternal truths of Islam. The missionaries, those other agents in the pay of the imperialists, are also working hard throughout the Islamic world in order to mislead our youth, not by converting them to their own faith, but by perverting them. This is, in fact, what the imperialists want to do: to corrupt. In Tehran itself, propaganda institutions have been created for the sole purpose of dragging the believers away from the truthful laws of Islam. Is it not our sacred duty to uproot this luring offspring of peril to Islam?

3

The Islamic Republic

An Islamic government can be neither dictatorial nor despotic. An Islamic government can only be constitutional and democratic. In this type of democracy, the laws are not made by the will of the people, but by the Koran and the tradition established by the Prophet [Sunna]. The constitution, the civil code, and the criminal code should be inspired only by Islamic principles contained in the Koran and transposed by the Prophet. Islamic government is the government of divine claim, and its laws can be neither replaced, nor altered in any way, nor disputed.

*

In any self-determined Islamic government worthy of trust, the legislative, the executive, and the judicial are to be replaced by a Divinity Planning Council. This council must keep every cabinet sector informed about the Islamic principles that relate to its activity, indicating what its agenda must be in accord with divine law. The council must also establish national policy, which must have at its core all the above-mentioned agendas.

*

The Islamic government is subject to the principles of Islam, which have been established neither by the people nor by its delegates, but directly by Allah and His divine will. Koranic law, which is based on these principles, is the core of any Islamic government and unswervingly presides over the entire population, which is, in fact, a part of it. The Prophet, the Caliphs [spiritual leaders], and the people must obey these everlasting laws made by God and handed down to humankind through the authority of the Koran and the Prophet, whose power shall not decrease until the end of days.

*

It is often claimed that the field of religion must be kept separated from that of politics, and that the clerics must not mix into any mundane affairs. It has been claimed that high ecclesiastical authorities must not interfere with the social and political decisions of the government. Such claims can be made only by atheists. They are conceived and propagated by imperialists. Yet, was ever politics segregated from religion in the time of the Prophet (may Allah bless him, him and his faithful followers!)? Was there a division at the time between the clerical and the political dignitaries? Were ecclesiastical and administrative powers separate in the time of the Caliphs? Those are deviations created by the imperialists in order to turn the clerics away from the material and social life of Islamists, and thus to get an uncontrolled hand to plunder their riches.

*

Hear this – a political clergy! And after all, why not? The Prophet used to be a politician!

*

The Prophet appointed provincial governors, created courts of law and named judges, opened embassies in foreign countries, and sent envoys to other tribes and rulers. He, in fact, organized all the structures of an ordinary government.

*

In order to unite all Islamists, to set the Islamic motherland free from the slavery enforced by the imperialists, we have no other choice but to form a genuine Islamic government, do whatever is needed to end the domination of all the other dictatorial pseudo-Islamic governments installed by infidels, and once this goal is reached to put in power the universal Islamic government.

*

We do not oppose going to the moon or building nuclear reactors. But we, too, have a mission to fulfill – the mission of serving the Islam and making its laws known to the whole world, hoping that all monarchs and presidents throughout the Islamic world will eventually admit that our duty is sacred, and in this way submit to our just cause. Of course, we have no intention to deprive them of their official roles. We shall allow them to stay in power as long as they are obedient and prove that they fully deserve our confidence.

*

If an enemy attacks the borders of an Islamic country, then it is the sacred mission of all Islamists in the world to defend it by every means possible, by giving their possessions, if necessary, or even their life. Nobody has to grant them official permission to accomplish this noble task.

*

If, within an Islamic country, satanic schemes conceived by alien minds are materialized, and if people fear that these might lead to foreign oppression, it is the sacred duty of every Islamist to vehemently oppose such schemes.

*

If, as a result of the political, economic, or mercantile domination imposed by some infidels, arise the risk of seeing the imperialists take control over the fate of Islamic countries, it is the responsibility of every Islamist to protect their sovereignty and fight against any foreign invasion.

*

If there are reasons to worry that the diplomatic relations of Islamic states with foreign ones might lead to the control of the latter over the former, even if such dominance be only political or economic, all Islamists must at any price combat this unfair situation, and force the Islamic governments to dissolve such iniquitous diplomatic relations.

*

If there is a justified fear that commercial relations with infidels might be detrimental to Islamic markets and create economic or mercantile dependency, such relations must be immediately terminated, and such commerce pronounced to be against Koranic law.

*

If instituting political or commercial relations between an Islamic and a non-Islamic country is not beneficial for Islam and Islamists, such relations are strictly prohibited. If a country establishes such disgraceful relations, it is the sacred mission of all Islamic countries to do whatever necessary to break off such unwanted relations.

*

If some leaders of Islamic countries or some members of parliament support a foreign political, economic, or military power, which is inexorably against the relevance of Islam and the benefit of all Islamists, they must be considered traitors and immediately stripped of their official duties, whatever they may be, even if their investitures have been performed according to the law. It is the sacred mission of all Islamists to rebuke and chastise these turncoats in any possible way.

*

It is prohibited for any Islamic country to have commercial and diplomatic relations with states which play the role of marionettes for the great powers – Israel, for example – and it is the duty of all Islamists to stand against such shameful relations by every possible means. That is why any entrepreneur who does business with Israel, its agents, or its delegates is a traitor to Islam and to all other Islamists, because he plays a part in the destruction of Islam. It is the sacred duty of all Islamists to break off their relations with such conspirators, whether they be official dignitaries or businessmen, with the purpose of compelling them to be remorseful.

*

All the laws endorsed and ratified so far by the two chambers of the Iranian Parliament, at the criminal suggestion of foreign infiltrators – may Allah chastise them! – violating the commandments of the Koran and the decrees of the Holy Prophet of Islam are hereby declared null and void from the Islamic standpoint. It is the duty of all believers to oppose all those who sustained them, to dodge their company and refrain from rubbing elbows with them, or do business with them, and to think of them as impure offenders. Indeed, even coming in their reach is in itself a serious transgression.

4

The Rule of the Religious Authorities

If religious authorities well versed in Koranic dogma and law dedicated themselves to the Islamic commandments and to establishing an Islamic state, never again would the people starve.

*

It is clearly written that "the religious authorities must rule the sultans." If the sultans obey the decrees of Islam, then they must also obey the clerics. The sultans must ask the clergy not only for laws and rules, but also for directions. In this way, the religious authorities are the true governors, and formally the power should always be in their hands.

*

You, the veritable religious authorities, have the sacred duty to set up an Islamic state. Do not give up self-reliance, because you are mighty enough to carry on your shoulders this heavy burden. We shall do what the imperialists did three or four centuries ago: they started from nothing, and look where they have gotten. We shall start from ground zero as well. Do not be daunted by a few co-nationals who have sold out to the infidels, who are the lackeys of Western colonialism. Let the people know that the clerics are not going to sit silently in a corner at Qom or An Najaf studying such puny subject-matters as the menstruation of women, or shutting themselves off from political issues simply because “religion and politics should not mix.”

*

Are the leaders of Islamic countries more competent than we are at present? Which of them rises above mediocrity? Many of them have never attended school…Mr. Reza [the Shah’s father] was a soldier of the lowest rank. Historically speaking, this has been the norm. Most dictators and tyrants had neither leadership skills, nor commonsensical coherence, nor understanding, nor insight. Harun al-Rashid [a famous Caliph of Baghdad in the 9th C.] or others like him, what did they accomplish in terms of education? In order to be able to promulgate laws and run a country, one needs to be highly educated.

*

In some instances, a subterfuge is required in order to keep the spirit of Islam, and of religion, in general, alive. Without subterfuges, faith cannot last for long.

*

If one who is after Islamic justice interprets the Koranic laws in a manner that contradicts the divine will, he is guilty of the sin of fabrication. All religious scholars must rebuke him, or else they themselves shall be rebuked.

*

Considering that the clerics have a lower status according to the hierarchy of Islam [than the Prophet and the Imam], does this imply that they should chastise an offender less rigorously? Can we say that the Prophet would have to order a hundred and fifty lashes, Ali a hundred, and the clergy only fifty, if the punishment should consist of one hundred lashes? No! The chief law officer must inflict as much punishment on a transgressor as it is demanded by the divine regulations, whether he be the Prophet, Ali, or one of their inferior representatives.

5

The Imam

We need a chief of government who is not the slave of his material desires and cravings. We need a leader to govern us in the spirit of equality and duty; a leader who rejects all kinds of favouritism, who sees his own family like any other family, who would chop off his son's hands if he stole, and who would have his brothers and sisters killed if they sold heroin.

*

As for the position and level of the investiture, one should notice that there is no difference between the guardian of a minor child and the guardian of an entire people. Indeed, heading a government or being in a leading position is even as the Imam and his assignees taking care of little children.

*

The great religious scholars, those strongholds of Islam, are not only the byword and epitome of Islamic belief, but also its keepers. They state Islamic truths in their poignant and touching sermons, and through the unique nature of their guiding mission. That is why, when after a long life, which may exceed a hundred years, they pass away, that demise is a huge loss for Islam. In such cases, all the faithful miss their overflowing presence. Thus, I have to think about my own death: who is going to miss me then, since all that I do now relates to sitting in a corner of my house where I study night and day?

*

The Imams were blazing flares in the darkness of the universe; their gifts were boundless; their innate qualities superior to all other humans. That is why the angel Gabriel stated, "If I stood too close to them [the Imams], they would scorch me."

*

The leaders of the Soviet Union, the United Kingdom, and the United States of America are endowed with power – even as the Imam – but they are heathens. They exert their political power and authority in order to pursue base personal goals, which they eventually achieve by promulgating callous laws and by making appeal to hardhearted political procedures. But the Imam and the clerics have the duty to make use of any political contraption to enforce the law of Allah and to establish an equalitarian system for the benefit of the entire people. Leadership means nothing for them but suffering and misery, and still what can they do? The government of the clergy is an obligation they must carry out.

*

Since Allah did not name anyone to form the Islamic government in the absence of the secreted Imam [the Twelfth Imam], what are we supposed to do? But while the Almighty did not designate anyone by name, He demanded that the righteous character of the members of the Islamic governments from the birth of Islam to the rule of the Twelfth Imam be propagated. This righteousness consists of several virtuous qualities such as perfect knowledge of Islamic law and justice, and should be looked for in many of the religious scholars of our time. If the erudite join forces, they will be able to set up the legitimate power that will establish widespread justice. If a worthy man who possesses all these matchless virtues emerges and forms a genuine Islamic government, it means that he has been invested by God with the same task as the Holy prophet, namely to govern the people. Hence, it is the people's sacred duty to follow him.

6

Islamic Justice

Under an Islamic regime, everyone is protected by the law. No one is permitted to threaten people's safety, break into their houses, arrest them with no reason, sentence them to prison, send them into exile, or summarily execute them on the grounds of an unverified charge or suspicion. Under an Islamic administration, all people can fully confide in the laws of the Prophet, and no magistrate or leader dare oppose them.

*

The individual who leads the Islamic society must always devote himself to its goals, not to his personal interests, putting his heart and soul into the community's welfare. That is why Islam has put to death so many people: to defend the goals and achievements of the Islamic society. Islam has wiped off many communities because they all generated corruption and endangered the wellbeing of Islamists.

*

Islamists are not allowed to seek restorations and remedies for their sorrows from the governments or from the courts of law that have not been constituted according to Islamic principles. They are not permitted to have legal recourse to monarchs or other totalitarian administrations, or to the magistrates who are appointed by them, even if they possess all the rights of defense provided by law. A person whose son has been murdered, or whose house has been broken into is forbidden to seek justice from such corrupt courts of law, even if he is in the right and has enough convincing evidence.

*

Islam has commandments for everything that relates to humans and society. These precepts come from Allah, and have been transmitted to men by His Prophet and Messenger. One might be awed by the splendour of these laws, which cover every aspect of life, from conception to committal. There is no field of human existence upon which Islam has not engraved the mark of its infinite justice and wisdom.

*

The Islamic republic is the sole form of government according to the Islamic law. Therefore, the learned men and religious scholars of the clergy are responsible for its safeguard. It is they who must oversee its government and organization. In applying the laws of God to such affairs as taxation and private property, for instance, they must be fully credible. At the same time, they must display no hesitancy in the execution of the Islamic laws. They must also be neither too merciful nor too cruel. If a cleric wishes to exact a chastisement on someone, he must do it in public, according to the long-established rules of Islam, and flog him the precise number of times required by the punishment of that offence, without verbally abusing him or slapping him or putting him in prison, even for a single day.

*

Islamic justice is based on nothing else but plainness and straightforwardness. It settles all criminal and civil complaints in the easiest, simplest, and fastest way possible. All that is needed is an Islamic judge with a pen and an inkwell, and two or three law enforcement officers. The judge is supposed to go to a place accompanied by the law enforcers, pass a verdict on any case, and see it put into effect. Just notice how expensive and time-consuming the Western-style judicial procedures are, all in the name of some principles which have nothing to do with Islam!

*

If the castigatory laws of Islam were implemented for only one year, all the distressing injustices and depravities would be deracinated. Immorality must be punished by the law of reprisal: chop off the hands of the thief; kill the murderer instead of imprisoning him; lash the adulterous man or woman. Your worries, your so-called "humanitarian" pangs of conscience display rather immaturity than rationality. Under the provisions of Koranic law, any magistrate meeting the seven conditions (he must have reached the age of puberty, be a true believer, know the Islamic laws by heart, be impartial, not be affected by memory loss, or be a bastard, or be of the female sex) is qualified to mete out justice in any legal dispute. Thus, he can judge and pass twenty verdicts in a single day, while the Western legal system might need several years in order to dispense of a similar number of trials.

*

Ali [Mohammed's son-in-law], after he had cut off the hands of two thieves, nursed their wounds and offered them his hospitality; this had such a great impact on them that they became his disciples. Some other time, when Ali heard that the pillaging army Muawiyah had taken advantage of a woman of one of the neighbouring tribes, he was so disturbed and so commiserated with her pain that he stated: "If a man lost his life after such a sorrowful event, no one could blame him." And yet, in spite of a disposition as sympathetic as his, Ali unsheathed his sword and gashed the abusers to pieces. This is the core of justice.

7

Youth

Students have opened their eyes wide. They can't wait to see the plan [of an Islamic republic] being materialized. Our students hate dictators, oppressive and imperialist authorities, the boors who plunder people's properties, and the impostors who intoxicate themselves. There are neither students nor universities that oppose an Islam founded on legitimate beliefs such as ours, and governed according to social ideologies such as ours.

*

Our youngsters have the sacred duty to remove and tear into shreds the turban worn by the hypocrites who pretend to be holy men and religious scholars. These frauds are producing so much corruption amongst Islamists! When I was young, it used to be different. Why don't they shred those turbans? I don't mean we should kill them; they do not deserve this privilege. But our brave youth must assure that such mullahs do not appear in public with the turban on their heads. There is no need to hit them too much, but those turbans must be taken off.

*

Abandon your pessimism and resignation! Develop your programs and improve your methods of spreading Islam! Focus more on the way you present these issues. Do your job well: be the brave pioneers of an

Islamic republic. Place your hands in the hands of those nations that fight for self-determination.

*

These days, all the boys and girls who have reached full sexual capacity are restrained from getting married simply because they are under age. This contravenes the intent of all divine laws. Why should, for example, the marriage of girls who have attained puberty be prohibited only because they are still "minors," when they are permitted to listen to the radio and to music that stimulates sexual desire?

*

You, young representatives of a new generation, please endeavour to perform an earnest mental exertion, and thus be more lucid in your reasoning. Do not turn to science alone, because its physical laws have caused so many of you to forget your main duties! Islam needs your help! Rescue the Islamists from their enemies! The missionaries of different religious groupings, who are all in the pay of the colonialists, exactly like their domestic agents, have extended their activities, being present in the four corners of the country, where they turn our youngsters away from the path of virtue and uprightness, and lead them far afield into activities that make them oblivious of the sacred interests of Islam. Save that youth!

8

Mass Media and Propaganda

Our duty is to create an Islamic republic, and in order to accomplish this task, we must first develop a network of propaganda. This is how things work – it's always been like that. Once a few persons sit down together, think about solutions together, and take decisions together, it means that a basic system of propaganda will surface. Then, one by one, others who share the same opinions will be attracted to the same group, and it will gradually increase in size. Eventually, the group and its propaganda machine will become a force that can paralyze the strong arm of an oppressive government, or even cause its slump and collapse.

*

Radio and television are permitted only if they are used for the broadcasting of news or materials for making the natural world and its marvels known to the public; yet, they must strictly forbid singing, music, the spreading of anti-Islamic principles, the praising of tyrants, lies of any kind, and shows which encourage skepticism and damage morality.

*

Since radio and TV sets are not used in compliance with the above-mentioned rules, their commercialization must be restricted to those who will put them to beneficial use, and who will make sure that others follow their example.

9

On How People Should Urinate and Defecate

When urinating or defecating, people should hide their genitals from all pubertal persons, even from their sisters and mothers, as well as from any children too young to understand and from any unintelligent person.

*

It is not required that one conceal his or her sexual organs with something; one's hand will suffice.

*

When defecating or urinating, one must squat in such a position in order to avoid both facing Mecca and turning one's back on it.

*

It is not enough to hide one's private parts by turning one's genitals away, while oneself facing or turning one's back on Mecca. At the same time, one's sex organs must never be uncovered either when looking in the direction of Mecca or when facing directly away from Mecca.

*

Urinating and defecating are prohibited in four places: dead ends, except when those who live in the area permit it; the private property of a person who has not allowed one to do so; places of veneration, such as theological schools [*medersas*]; graves of believers, unless one does so as an affront to their memory.

*

It is mandatory to cleanse one's anus with water in three instances: when the excrement has been driven out with other impurities, such as blood; when something contaminated has scuffed the anus; when the anal orifice has been smeared more than usual in the act of defecation. Apart from these three instances, one may want to purify one's anus with water or wipe it with some cloth or a stone.

*

The urinary opening should be cleaned with water only, and it is sufficient to wash it once after urinating. But those who urinate through some other orifice should wash that opening at least two times. This is valid for women too.

*

It is not necessary to wipe one's anus with three stones or three cloths; one stone or one cloth should suffice. But if one wipes it with a bone or with a sacred object, such as a piece of paper with the name of Allah on it, this person must not pray while in this state.

*

It is recommended that for urinating or defecating one squat down in a hidden place. One should step into this isolated place with the left foot first, and step out with the right foot first. It is preferable to move bowels with the head covered, and to balance the body on the left foot while in this position.

*

During defecation, one is not allowed to squat facing the sun or the moon, unless one's sex organs are well covered. While evacuating, one must also avoid squatting in the direction of the wind, in public places, at the door of one's house, or under a fruit tree. At the time of a bowel movement, one should not eat, dally, or clean one's anus with the right hand. Last but not least, one must keep quiet, unless one is forced to speak, or is praying to Allah.

*

It is preferable to avoid urinating standing up, or urinating onto a hard surface, or into an animal lair, or into water, especially still water.

*

It is recommended that one avoid holding back the need to urinate or defecate, especially if this necessity becomes hurtful.

*

It is highly recommended that one urinate before saying prayers, before going to bed, before having sexual intercourse, and after reaching orgasm.

*

After urination, a man must first clean his anus if it has been dripped by urine. Then, one must push three times with his middle finger of the left hand on the area between the anus and the base of the penis. After that, one must place his thumb on top of the penis and his index finger on the bottom, and pull the skin forward three times as far as the circumcision ring; and then, he must squeeze three times the frontal part of the penis.

*

A woman has no special instructions to follow after urination. If she notices some moisture around the vagina, which she does not know whether it is pure or impure, that moisture is to be considered pure, and in no way can it refrain her from performing ablutions or saying prayers.

10

On How People Should Eat and Drink

There are eighteen rules to follow at mealtimes: one must wash one's hands before the meal; one must wash and dry one's hands after the meal; the master of the house must begin eating before the guests, and must always finish after them; the master of the house must be the first to wash his hands before the meal; the master of the house must be followed by the guest who sits at his right, and then the next, and so on, until reaching the person sitting at his left; one must begin the meal by praising Allah; if more than one course is served, it is recommended that one invoke the name of Allah before every course; one must take food with the right hand only; one must eat with three fingers, leaving the other two free; one must also avoid ingurgitation; one must extend the period of time allotted for the meal as much as possible; one must masticate the food properly; one must praise Allah at the end of the meal; one must lick one's fingers; one must clean one's teeth after the meal with a toothpick, which must not be made of pomegranate wood, basil wood, reed, or palm leaves; one must collect the leftovers in order to eat them later, but if the food is eaten in the desert it is recommended that one leave the leftovers for the birds and animals of the desert; one must eat at sunrise and at sunset, and stay away from food during the day and during the night; one must lie down and rest by putting the right leg over the left one; one must eat salt at the beginning and at the end of every meal; one must wash all fruit well before eating it.

*

There are eleven misconducts that one must recoil from when eating. Here is what must be shunned at mealtimes: one must not eat when not hungry; one must not be greedy, for eating too much displeases Allah; one must refrain from watching others while eating; one must not eat food which is too hot; one must not blow onto a plate or into a glass to help the food or drink cool faster; one is not allowed to start eating as soon as the bread has been laid on the table; one is forbidden to cut bread with a knife; one must not put bread under one's plate; one must avoid eating all the meat from a bone, and make sure that there are a few remnants left on it; one must refrain from peeling fruit; one must not throw away partially eaten fruit.

*

There are six rules to follow while drinking water: one must rather draw the water out of the recipient with the lips, at the same time avoiding to gulp it down; one must drink water standing straight upward, reciting the name of Allah before and after drinking; one must drink water in three phases; one must drink water because one wants to, and not because one is forced to; one must evoke the martyrdom of Hazrat Aba

Abdullah and his family, and curse their slayers after drinking.

*

There are five restrictions concerning the drinking of water: one must not drink too much; one must not drink after a copious meal; one must refrain from drinking water standing up during the night; one is forbidden to hold the water jug in the left hand; one must not drink from a chipped or broken area of the jug or from a place close to the handle.

*

Among the organs of domesticated animals or game beasts, birds, fish, and so on, whose meat you are allowed to eat, there are fifteen which are banned: blood; excrement; the penis; the vagina; the uterus; the glands; the testicles; the core of the brain; the tiny chickpea-shaped ball at the back side of the brain; the nerves located on the two sides of the spine; the gallbladder; the liver; the bladder; the eyes; and the meat from under the claws.

*

It is strictly prohibited to eat the excrement of animals or their mucus. But if it so happens that little fragments of excrement or mucus are absorbed into other foods, their eating is not prohibited.

*

The meat of horses, mules, or donkeys is not recommended.

This meat becomes stringently forbidden if a man sodomized the animal before it was slaughtered. In such a case, the animal must be taken out of the city and put up for sale.

*

If one sodomizes a cow, a ewe, or a camel, its urine and excrement always become contaminated, and even its milk becomes impure, being improper for drinking. The animal must be killed as soon as possible and burned, while the man who has committed the act of sodomy must pay the owner its price.

*

The drinking of wine or alcoholic beverages constitutes a mortal sin, and is strictly prohibited. One who drinks alcohol maintains only a part of his soul, namely that part which is distorted and evil; this person is damned by the Almighty, His archangels, His prophets, and His believers. The prayers of a person who has consumed alcohol are rejected by Allah for a period of forty days. On the very day of the resurrection of the death, this person's face will grow black, his tongue will jut out of his mouth, his saliva will flow down his chest, and his thirst will never be quenched.

11

Cleanness and Uncleanness

There are eleven things which are unclean: urine, excrement, sperm, bones, blood, dogs, pigs, non-Islamists, wine, beer, and the sweat of the camel which eats excrement.

*

The urine and excrement of humans and any animal whose blood gushes out when a vein or artery of its body is cut open are unclean. Yet, flyspecks or waste materials discharged from mosquitoes or any small insects whose blood does not spurt are clean.

*

The urine and excrement of any dejection-eating animal are impure. This is also valid for the urine and excrement of any animal used for sexual gratification by a human being, and also for the urine and excrement of sheep fed on sow's milk.

*

The seminal fluid of any animal whose blood gushes out, when its throat is cut open, is unclean.

*

The bones of an animal which has been found dead or which has not been slaughtered according to Islamic rules are unclean. Fish, on the other side, can never be unclean, even when found dead in the water, and that is because its blood does not gushes out.

*

The hairs, bones, and teeth of dead animals are clean as long as they are not from animals which are unclean because of their nature, such as dogs.

*

An egg taken from the entrails of a chicken is not to be considered unclean as long as its shell is not broken. Nevertheless, such an egg must be diligently washed before being eaten.

*

The meat, fat, and skins one buys from an Islamic souk or from an Islamist are clean as long as such items for consumption do not come from animals which were not slaughtered according to the Islamic precepts.

*

The blood of any human or animal whose blood gushes out when the throat is cut open is unclean. On the other side, the blood of the fish, mosquito, or any other creature whose blood does not spurt is clean.

*

The blood that may come out from the space between one's teeth is clean only if mixed with saliva: that saliva may indeed be swallowed. Clotted blood amassed under the nails or in any other part of the body is clean if its exterior has been so transformed that one cannot say it is blood any longer; if that is not so, one must do whatever necessary in order to get rid of it before performing the ablutions.

*

The pus of a wound in the process of healing is clean, but one has to make sure it does not contain any blood.

*

Dogs and pigs are unclean, except for those living in the water. Their hairs, bones, claws, and excrements are also unclean. Yet, sea dogs and sea pigs are clean.

*

Each part of the body of non-Islamists is unclean, including the hair on their hands, legs and torso, their nails, and all their discharged fluids.

*

Any man or woman who disallows the existence of Allah, or believes in the so-called equals of the Almighty [the Christian Trinitarian form of God], or does not have faith in the words revealed to the Prophet Mohammed, is unclean (in a similar manner to feces, urine, dogs, and the drinking of wine). A person is unclean even if he only has reservations about these precepts.

*

A child who has not yet reached puberty is unclean if his parents and grandparents are not Islamists; but if the child has at least one Islamist among his ancestors, then he is clean.

*

An Islamist who offends or opposes one of the Twelve Imams is unclean.

*

Wine and all the other alcoholic beverages are unclean, but opium and hashish are not.

*

Beer is unclean, but the brewer's yeast is clean.

*

The sweat of an animal which eats its own excrement is unclean, whereas the sweat of other animals, which do not eat their dejections, is clean.

*

The sweat of a man who has recently ejaculated is not unclean. Nevertheless, it is recommendable that he not pray as long as his body or garments preserve the moisture of the sweat.

*

If a man has performed sexual intercourse with his wife during the established periods of abstinence, such as the Ramadan fast, he must abstain from saying his prayers as long as his skin retains the moisture of the postcoital sweat.

*

If a part of the body that is sweating comes into physical contact with an unclean thing, and the sweat runs down to other parts of the body, all those parts become unclean, while the rest of the body stays clean.

*

Mucus and expectorations which contain blood are unclean, but those without blood are clean. If the mucus or expectoration comes into contact with the nose or mouth even sparingly, the part of the skin which has been touched must be cleansed. Yet, the untouched part stays clean.

*

An object which penetrates the body of a person, and by doing so is soiled by something unclean, such as feces or blood, remains clean when removed from that body if the object contains no deposits of the unclean substance accumulated on it. For example, the enema tube which is introduced into the patient's rectum or the scalpel of a surgeon is not unclean if it has no deposits of such residues. The same rule applies to saliva or mucus which combines with blood inside the mouth or nose, but displays no trace of blood when expectorated.

*

It is strictly forbidden to touch a page of the Koran with anything that is unclean. Yet, if this happens, the page must be cleaned immediately.

*

It is prohibited to put on the Koran any unclean material such as blood, or human or animal bones if the substance is dried. In case the material has already been put on the Koran, it must be removed at once.

*

It is forbidden to write out verses of the Koran with unclean ink; writing even a single letter with unclean ink is a great offence. Should this already have been done, it must be washed away or expunged with a knife or another sharp instrument.

*

One must not give the Koran to an unbeliever. It is highly recommended that one use any means, including force if needed, in order to take the Koran away from the infidel who has it in his hands.

*

In case a page of the Koran or a piece of paper which has on it the name of the Almighty, or the Prophet, or one of the Imams happens to fall into a toilet, one must remove it from there at any cost. If this proves to be impossible, the toilet must not be used again until one determines that the paper has fully disintegrated.

*

It is strictly forbidden to eat or drink anything that is unclean. It is also prohibited to give anything unclean to children to eat, regardless of its potential to harm their health. Yet, it is permitted to serve children food which has indirectly come into contact with an unclean thing.

*

One may abstain from pointing out to a person that he is having unclean food or that he is praying while wearing unclean garments.

*

In case the head of the family spots during the course of a meal that one or more of the dishes being served are unclean, he must inform all his guests about this; but if it is one of the guests who notices the unclean dish, he may or may not do the same thing.

12

On Cleansing

There are eleven substances and methods which cleanse, that means which are able to expunge adulteration and make bodies and objects clean again: water; earth; sun; transformation; diminution of the amount of grape juice by two-thirds; blood transfer; Islam; interdependence; elimination of all unclean objects; forbidding an excrement-eating animal to eat its own dejection for a certain period of time; absence of the Islamist. This is the purport of each substance and method:

Water cleanses if it meets the following requirements: it is clean (that is why watermelon juice and rose water do not cleanse); it contains no impurities; when used to wash something unclean, it has not been contaminated by the odour, colour, or taste of that unclean substance; after such washing, the remnants of feces or other residues have left no traces in its composition.

An unclean dish or container must be washed three times in order to be clean again; yet, a container which has been licked by a dog or which has been used for giving food or water to a dog must be chafed with earth before being washed twice in water. If a pig has used it, the container must be washed seven times in a row, but there is no need to chafe it with earth. A cup or glass in which there has been wine, and as a consequence is unclean, must be washed three times, although it is by far better to wash it seven times. An oven which has become unclean because one has urinated in it recovers its cleanness after being filled with sufficient water in order to cover all its sides, not only once, but twice. But if the oven has become unclean because it has been soiled by a different substance, such as feces, filling it with water once, after having removed the filth, will suffice. If something becomes unclean as a result of having come into contact with the urine of a boy who has been fed milk (who is less than two), who has not drunk sow's milk, washing it all over once will suffice. Yet, it is more prudent to wash it again a second time. If the surface of a grain of wheat or rice or a cake of soap comes into contact with some unclean matter, immersing it into the prescribed quantity of water required for cleansing will normally suffice; but if the uncleanness has entered into its substance, this method of cleansing is insufficient. Yet, if one is not sure whether the filth has penetrated deeply into it or not, then the soap is considered to be clean. Any unclean object becomes clean only when the unclean part has been entirely removed from its corpus; but if the odour or colour of the unclean part remains, it makes no difference at all. The tiny fragments of food that remain between one's teeth after having a meal become clean if one washes his mouth with water in such a way that all the unclean bits are washed away.

If lump sugar has been produced from unclean melted sugar, the lump sugar stays unclean even when placed in water, whether it is running or still.

Earth cleanses the sole of one's foot or shoe when it comes into contact with something unclean, if it meets the following three requirements: it is clean; it is dry; and there is enough of it to eliminate the unclean substance (such as blood, urine, feces, etc.) from the sole of the foot.

The earth may be muddy, solid, sandy, or pebbly. Walking on a rug, carpet, or grass to cleanse the sole of the foot or shoe is not enough; walking on asphalt or floors will not suffice either.

To cleanse the sole of the foot or shoe which came into contact with an unclean object, one must take at least fifteen steps, regardless of whether the filth has disappeared before the fifteen steps are completed or not.

For those who crawl on their hands or knees, fifteen steps are insufficient to cleanse their palms or their knees after they have come into contact with something unclean. This rule also applies to canes, crutches, horseshoes, wagon wheels, etc. If small fragments of feces or other filth remain after the fifteen steps have been taken, they must be carefully eliminated.

Their odour and colour will still persist, but this makes no difference at all. The inner side of the shoe, or the part of the sole of the foot which does not touch the ground will not be cleansed simply by taking a certain number of steps. The same principle applies to socks, unless the part of the sock which covers the sole of the foot is made of leather or hide.

Sun has cleansing power over unclean substances, such as the ground, buildings, doors, windowpanes, or nails hammered into walls, if the following six requirements are met: the unclean object must be moist (in case it is dry, the object must be moistened, so the sun may dry it); the unclean part must be eliminated before the object is exposed to the sunbeams; the sunbeams must not be sieved through a curtain or through clouds, for instance (very thin clouds do not count); the unclean object must be dried exclusively by the sun, and never by a combination of sun and wind; the rays of the sun must dry all of the unclean part of a building at one time (cleansing the façade of the building first, and the other walls only later is not acceptable); one must make sure that the structure of the wall contains no outside particles, for example air. In case the sun has dried out unclean ground, but later it is not clear whether at the time the ground was moist or dry, or whether its moisture dried exclusively because of the sun or because of other causes, that ground is to be considered unclean; the same rule applies to ground or a building about which one is not sure whether the unclean parts were eliminated from it before it was exposed to the rays of the sun, or whether the sun shed its beams directly upon it. If only one of the walls was exposed to the sun, the other walls stay unclean, unless the wall is so thin that when it dries, the other walls will dry too.

Transformation is a process through which an unclean substance is so fully changed that it turns into something clean. For example, after the unclean wood has burned, it becomes clean ashes; or a dead dog which has been buried in saline ground transforms into clean salt. Yet, this principle does not apply to unclean wheat which is made into flour or bread. Wine which becomes vinegar, whether by itself or by addition of salt or vinegar, is clean, but vinegar resulting from wine made of grapes which have come into contact with urine or feces, or from wine which contains such dejections, remains clean. Vinegar made with unclean grapes, raisins, or dates stays unclean. Raisins transformed into vinegar are accepted, and so is the vinegar which may contain straws, small fragments of vine, or tiny bits of date tree. There is no objection either if cucumbers or egg-plants are added to the dates, raisins, or grapes that are to be transformed into vinegar.

Reducing the quantity of grape juice by two-thirds guarantees the validity of the cleansing process. Boiled grape juice is not unclean even before its reduction by two-thirds, but its drinking is prohibited if proven to be intoxicating; in this case, the juice becomes pure only if it is transformed into vinegar. The juice of an unripe cluster of grapes, even if the cluster has one or two ripe grapes on it, may be drunk provided that it is first boiled and that the sweetness of the grape has completely disappeared.

Blood transfer is the procedure through which the blood of a human or an animal (whose blood gushes when its throat is cut open) becomes clean when transferred into the body of an insect (whose blood does not spurt), and is absorbed into the blood of the latter. On the other side, human blood sucked by a leech preserves its uncleanness even after its transfer into the body of the leech because it is not absorbed into the blood of the leech.

In case a human being crushes a mosquito on his skin without being able to establish whether the blood on that spot belongs to the insect or to himself, then this blood is to be considered clean; but if the time between the mosquito bite and the death of the mosquito is so short that one cannot distinguish between the two, then the blood is clean.

Islam. A non-Islamist, whether a man or a woman, who converts to Islam, automatically receives a clean body, plus clean saliva, mucus, and perspiration. As for the converts' attire, if it comes into contact with their sweat before they convert to Islam, then it stays unclean.

Interdependence means the cleansing of an unclean object being subject to the cleansing of another unclean object. In the case of the wine which is turned into vinegar, the container which has held the wine becomes clean once more up to the level reached by the wine which has already become vinegar. In this way, the piece of wood or stone on which funerary ablutions are performed, the material covering the genitals of the deceased, the hand of the person who has made the ablutions, and the soap with which the dead body was washed become clean once the ablution has been completed.

The body of an animal or insect which has come into direct contact with an unclean element, blood for example, or into indirect contact with unclean water, becomes cleansed again as soon as the unclean substance is removed. The same rule applies to the inner part of one's mouth or nose. Thus, if an insignificant quantity of blood runs out between one's teeth and dissolves in saliva, there is no need to wash one's mouth; but if one's denture has come into contact with some unclean matter, it must be taken out and washed. In case small fragments of food remain between one's teeth and the inner part of one's mouth starts to bleed, these fragments of food are clean as long as one is not aware that the blood has come into contact with them.

Forbidding an excrement-eating animal to eat its own dejection for a certain period of time. The urine and excrement of such an animal are unclean, and that is why in order for them to become clean, these animals must be restricted from eating human feces for the following period of time: forty days for a camel; twenty days for a cow or bull; ten days for sheep; seven or five days for a turkey; and three days for a chicken.

Absence of the Islamist. In case the clothes, kitchen utensils, or carpets belonging to an Islamist have come into contact with some unclean element while their owner is absent, they may not automatically be considered to be unclean as long as one is not certain that they were not washed and cleansed before he left, or that they did not accidentally fall into running water, which in reality cleansed them.

If one is sure that an object contaminated by some unclean substance has been cleansed, or if two trusty persons bear witness that it has, that object becomes clean again. This is also valid for an object about which its owner avows that it has been cleansed or that an Islamist has washed it, even if it is impossible to make sure that he did so according to the established rule.

*

One must refrain from eating or drinking from any container made of pig skin or dog hide, or from any container made from animal bones.

*

The leftover food of dogs, pigs, and non-Islamist men and women is unclean. The leftover food of animals whose flesh may be eaten is not unclean, but it is recommended that one refrain from consuming it.

13

On Water

There are two types of water: clean and unclean. The latter is mixed with other substances, for example watermelon juice, extract of roses, or muddied waters. Clean water is classified into five categories: still water which is large enough in order to be cleansed; still water in small quantities; running water; rainwater; and well water.

*

Cleansing water [*kor*] is the quantity of water held by a container whose length, width and depth are 3 ½ *vadjab* [approx. 70 centimetres or 27 inches]. This quantity of water should have 128 *maund*, minus 20 *miskal* [approx. 390 kilograms or 860 pounds].

*

In case the above-mentioned water changes its taste, odour, or colour because it has come into contact with such impurities as blood or urine, it becomes unclean; but if it modifies its taste, odour, or colour in an indirect way, because of an impure agent – for instance, if its odour is changed because of the propinquity of some form of decomposing substance – it still remains clean.

*

Water which has been contaminated by blood, urine, or other filth, and as a consequence has modified its odour, colour, or taste, can only be cleansed by running water or by rainwater which either falls straight into it, or is driven into it by the power of the wind, or is borne to it by a drainpipe, thus recovering its cleansing quality.

*

Whether a certain amount of water is sufficient for cleansing may be determined as follows: either through one's firm belief that it is, or by two reliable men avowing that it is.

*

The water used for washing the end of the urinary tract and the anus preserves its cleanness in five instances: if it has neither the odour, nor the colour, nor the taste of urine or excrement; if no external filth has soiled it; if no other unclean element such as blood comes out from the anus or the end of the urinary tract when defecating or urinating; if no specks of feces or urine can be noticed in the water; if the feces that has come into contact with the anus has not been released in an excessive quantity.

*

Running water, even though in a smaller amount than that of cleansing water, stays clean, and consequently drinkable, if it contains feces or urine, but only in case the combination of these substances has not modified its odour, colour, or taste.

*

If feces, urine, or other filth has contaminated running water, only the part which has altered its odour, colour, or taste becomes unclean, the rest of it remaining clean.

*

If there is any excrement, urine, or any other filth on the roof of a house when it is raining, the rainwater preserves its purity only in case it falls continuously off the roof, directly on the ground, or down a gutter or drainpipe. Yet, if the rain stops, the water which continues to run off is unclean because of its contact with the unclean matter existent on the roof.

14

On Ablution

There are two types of ablutions: one that is performed one step at a time, and another that is performed as a whole. The former consists of washing the parts of the body one by one, and the latter consists of immersing the entire body in water.

*

In the first type of ablution, one must proceed by declaring in both a loud and a low voice that one is going to perform the ablutions. After that, one must wash one's head, the back of the neck, the right side of the body, and then the left side. In case this strict order is not accurately followed, whether willingly or unwillingly, the ablutions are invalid. One should also be aware that the right side of the navel and the right side of the genitals must be washed with the right side of the body, while the left side of the navel and genitals must be washed with the left side of the body. Yet, it is wise that one wash all the surface of the navel and genitals along with each side of the body. If one discovers that one part of the body has been missed out once the ablution is completed, the ablution ritual must be repeated. In this case, if the missed-out part is on the left side of the body, washing only that part will suffice, but if it is on the right side of the body, after having washed that part, the entire left side of the body must be washed one more time.

*

In a full ablution, one must immerse the whole body in water, after having declared in both a loud and a low voice that one is going to perform the ablution. If one notices, after the ablution is completed, that some part of the body was left outside the water, even though one does not know precisely which part of the body it was, the whole ablution ritual must be performed again.

*

It is essential that during ablution all the parts of the body be carefully washed. However, it is not necessary that one wash those parts which cannot be seen, for example the inside of the ears or nose. If the ears are pierced, the holes in them must be washed if they are large enough in order to make the insides visible; otherwise, this is not required.

*

Although during ablution one must wash the shortest hairs on the body, it is advisable that one wash the longest hairs too. If one plans to wash his anus in the water of a public bath, one must first be granted permission by the owner of the bath, otherwise the ablution is invalid. If, during the ablution ritual, one releases intestinal gases or urinates, the ablution is still valid. If one performs his ablutions after he has ejaculated, and one has a verse of the Koran or the name of God written or tattooed on his body, one must keep his hand away from that spot during the ablution ritual; yet, that part of the body must be washed too, but without being touched.

*

Sperm is always unclean, whether it is released during a sexual act or in an involuntary act, while a man is either awake or asleep, whether it is in great quantities or small, whether it results from actual coitus or not, whether the discharge is deliberate or not.

*

It is recommended that a man always urinate after having ejaculated. If one does not urinate after he has ejaculated, the release that may follow one's ablution will be considered to be sperm, even though one is not sure about its true nature.

*

During the sexual act, if the penis penetrates a woman's vagina or a man's anus, either fully or only up to the circumcision ring, both partners become unclean, even if they have not reached the age of puberty. That is why they must perform their ablutions.

*

If the man considers that he has not penetrated the woman's vagina beyond the circumcision ring, ablution is not necessary.

*

If a man – may Allah prevent him from it! – has sexual intercourse with an animal and ejaculates, ablution is mandatory.

*

If the sperm moves within the penis without being released, or if one is not sure whether the sperm was actually discharged, ablution is not required.

*

A man who has ejaculated and has not performed his ablutions yet must steer clear of the following ten activities: eating; drinking; reading more than seven verses of the Koran; touching the binding of the holy Koran, the margin of its pages, or the spaces between the lines; carrying the Koran on him;

sleeping; dyeing his beard with henna; anointing himself with grease or oil; having sex after he has ejaculated in his sleep.

*

If a man becomes sexually intimate with his wife during the periods of time when he is required to be abstinent – for example during the Ramadan, when people must fast for a month – this man's sweat is unclean and he is restricted from saying his daily prayers while in this impure condition.

*

If a man becomes sexually excited by the view of a woman other than his wife, and as a result of this arousal he has sexual intercourse with his own wife, it is recommended that he not pray in case he has sweated; yet, if he first has intercourse with his wife and then with another woman, he is allowed to say his daily prayers even though he has sweated.

*

A man who has ejaculated while having sexual intercourse with a woman other than his wife, and who then ejaculates again as a result of being intimate with his wife, is prohibited from saying his daily prayers while still in a sweat; but, in case this man has had coitus with his wife first and then with a woman other than his wife, he is permitted to say his prayers while still sweating.

*

If a fly or another insect perches on an unclean object that is moist and then on a clean object that is moist, the latter becomes unclean too, but only if one is absolutely sure that the former was unclean; unless one is certain of its impurity, that object is to be considered clean.

*

Besides the ablutions that are mandatory, there are other ablutions which are very pleasant to Allah, and that is why they are strongly recommended. Here are a few:

Ablution performed on a Friday between dawn and noon.

Ablution performed on the eve of the first day of Ramadan and the eves of all the odd days of that particular month (for example, the third, fifth, seventh, and so on). The ablutions on the eves of the first, the fifteenth, the seventeenth, the nineteenth, the twenty-first, the twenty-third, the twenty-fifth, the twenty-seventh, and the twenty-ninth days of Ramadan are highly recommended. It is also recommended that on the eve of the twenty-third day the believer perform two ablutions: one at the beginning of the night and the other at its end.

Ablution performed by a woman who has used perfume for a man other than her husband.

Ablution of the man who has fallen asleep drunk.

Ablution of a man or woman who, during a total eclipse of the sun or the moon, has not said his or her established prayers.

Ablution of one who has witnessed the hanging of a

person sentenced to death. In case this person was forced to witness the hanging, ablution is not mandatory.

15

On the Five Daily Prayers

One must say his five daily prayers [*namaz*] in a state of maximum concentration and deep contemplation. This person must refrain from committing such transgressions as those of envy, conceit, trouble-starting, or eating prohibited foods, drinking alcohol, or refusing to pay his tithes to the clerics. It is also advisable that he refrain from committing such terrible transgressions as saying his daily prayers while half asleep or holding back his urine; one is also forbidden to look up at the sky during the act of praying. On the other side, it is recommended that one wear agate rings on his fingers, that he is appropriately dressed and properly combed, that his teeth are well brushed, and that he wear perfume.

*

While he is saying his five daily prayers, a man must make sure that his genitals and behind are well covered, even if they cannot be seen by anybody. It is recommended that he cover the entire part of the body from the navel to the knees.

*

A woman, while performing her five daily prayers, must cover properly the whole body, including her head and hair; yet, she is allowed to leave uncovered a part of her face, hands, and feet up to the ankles.

*

In case a man discovers, while performing one of his daily prayers, that his penis is uncovered, he must cover it at once; if that takes too long, he must end his prayer and start all over again. However, in case he notices only after he has finished the prayer that his penis is uncovered, the prayer is to be considered legitimate.

*

During the act of praying, it is allowed to cover one's body and genitals with grass or leaves, but it is advisable that one stick to this extreme method only when there are no other possibilities left.

*

During collective prayer, the woman must place herself behind the man. In case the woman and the man enter the mosque at the same moment and the woman is in front of the man, she must say her prayer once again after positioning herself where her place is, that means behind the man.

*

It is essential that one avoid sitting at the same table with one who does not attend a place of worship. One must never ask the advice of such a person; he must also refuse to live close to him, marry a woman from his family, or allow his daughter to marry him.

*

It is prohibited to say one's prayers in the following places: a bathroom; salty ground; facing a person; facing an open door; on a highway, road or street; in front of a fireplace or source of light; in the kitchen or any other place where there is an oven; before a well or cesspit; facing a picture or statue of a living personality, unless these are well covered; in the company of a man who has ejaculated and has not performed his ablutions; in a room in which there is a photograph, even if it does not face the person who is praying; in front of a tomb or on a tomb, or between two tombs in a graveyard.

*

A retarded person, a child, or one who has just eaten garlic must not be allowed into the mosque.

*

A person who has fallen asleep during the act of praying must say the prayer once again if he knows for sure that he dozed while saying it. In case this person is not certain whether he dozed or not, the prayer is to be considered legitimate.

*

Coughing, belching loudly, or sighing does not make a prayer void. However, the prayer becomes invalid if one utters interjections comprising at least two letters.

*

If the face of a person who is saying a prayer turns red because of stifling a shriek of laughter, he must repeat the prayer from the beginning.

*

In case one sobs audibly while praying because of some worldly distress, the prayer becomes void. Nevertheless, if one wails to oneself, the prayer is legitimate. Yet, if one sobs aloud because of the fear of the Almighty or the hereafter, this person is to be given strong confidence to wail.

*

If one claps one's hands or jumps up in the air during the act of praying, the prayer is invalidated.

*

If one swallows tiny fragments of food left over between one's teeth during prayer, the prayer is not voided. However, in case one has a piece of sugar in one's mouth and the sugar gradually melts during the prayer, the validity of the prayer is questionable.

*

During the act of praying, one must avoid by all means bending one's head to the right or to the left, closing one's eyes, clasping one's hands, spitting, playing with one's beard, looking at the writings of the Koran or any other writings, or at the motif of a ring. One must also avoid praying when feeling sleepy, when needing to urinate or defecate, or when one is wearing socks that are too tight.

16

On Prayers to Be Said in Case of Unrest Produced By Natural Phenomena

Namazeayat is the name of the prayer that must be said in case of natural phenomena which produce unrest. This prayer is to be said in four instances: when there is a total or partial eclipse of the sun; when there is a total or partial eclipse of the moon; in case of an earthquake, even though not scary; in case of a thunderstorm with lightning, and black or red winds.

*

If some of these phenomena take place simultaneously, for example if an eclipse is accompanied by an earthquake, one must say two prayers.

*

If there is an earthquake, or a thunderstorm with lightning, one must pray at once. One who does not pray under these circumstances commits a transgression which is not forgiven until one says this prayer, no matter how long after that, even on the last day of one's life.

*

In case a woman is having her period during a solar or lunar eclipse, no prayer for this natural phenomenon is needed until the eclipse is over. Nor is it mandatory for her to say the prayer at a later time.

17

On Fasting

Coitus must be considered a breaking of the fast, even if the penis does not penetrate the vagina deeper than the circumcision ring, and even if there is no sperm release.

*

If the penis penetrates the vagina less deeply than the circumcision ring, and there is no sperm release, the fast remains intact.

*

In case a man is not sure how deep the penis has penetrated the vagina, and if his penis has entered into the vagina beyond the circumcision ring, the fast has not been broken.

*

If a man has forgotten that he is in a fasting period and has sexual intercourse, or if he is forced to have sexual intercourse, his fast remains intact. However, if he remembers that he is in a fasting period while he is engaged in the coitus, or in case he is no longer forced to have intercourse, he must stop this illegitimate activity at once.

*

If a man brings himself to ejaculation by manual stimulation during a fasting period, his fast becomes invalid.

*

If a man releases sperm involuntarily, his fast has not been broken. However, if the ejaculation, even though not desired, is somehow caused by one of his acts, the fast is to be considered illegitimate.

*

The act of taking an enema, even for medical reasons, during a fasting period, makes the fast null; yet, suppositories are permitted, except for those containing opium, which are not recommended.

*

The fast of one who bears false witness – in thought, word, or deed – against Allah, His Prophet, or His disciples, is instantaneously voided, even if this person admits right away that he or she has lied, and honestly repents. One is also forbidden to blaspheme the holy name of Fatima [Mohammed's daughter, and Ali's wife], along with the sacred name of the other prophets and their disciples.

*

If, during the fasting period, one sincerely ascribes a quotation to the Almighty or to His Prophet, and he afterwards discovers that it was an erroneous attribution, the fast has not been broken. However, in case one deliberately ascribes a statement to Allah, to His Prophet, or to the Prophet's disciples, the fast becomes invalid. Yet, if one is only reiterating such an assertion heard from another person, the fast does not lose its validity.

*

The fast becomes null in case one immerses his entire head under water, but if one places only the right side and then the left side under water, the fast remains legitimate. One's head must never be plunged under rose water; yet, it may be immersed in other liquids, no matter whether they contain water or not.

*

If, during a period of fasting, one plunges his entire head under water in order to save somebody from drowning, his fast is voided, even if there was no other way of rescuing that person.

*

If a man who has ejaculated does not complete the established ablution rituals during the vigil of the month of Ramadan, the fast is broken.

*

If, before a Ramadan vigil, one considers that he will have sufficient time to perform his ablutions after he has ejaculated, but realizes that he does not have time to complete the rituals, he is permitted to defer his ablutions in order to commence the fast.

*

In case a fly enters the mouth of a person during a period of fasting, it is not mandatory for him to take it out, if the fly has not advanced too far into the throat; if the insect has gotten stuck in the throat, he must take it out at all costs, even if that makes him vomit, and thus the fast loses its legitimacy.

*

If one eats something during the fast without realizing what he is doing, and notices only afterwards what he has done, this person must not try to take out the food which has already been swallowed.

*

The following practices are not recommended during a period of fasting: putting drops in one's eyes; having a blood transfusion or taking a bath; pinching snuff or smelling fragrant plants; taking sitz bath (applies only to women); taking suppositories; getting one's clothes wet; having teeth extracted or undergoing oral surgery which could cause blood to flow into one's mouth; brushing one's teeth with a damp wood; engaging in amorous games with one's wife, even without the intention of having an orgasm, or deliberately exciting oneself (if one ejaculates, the fast becomes null and void).

18

On Women and Their Periods

A woman who bleeds from her uterus via the vagina, at a different time than that of her regular periods, is not menstruating. The discharge may be yellowish, cold, and thin. The blood may be released without any stinging sensation, and may also be blackish or yellow, hot, dense, and cause a stinging sensation when discharged.

*

False menses are of three types: mild, medium, and severe. If the blood which has been discharged does not entirely soak a piece of cotton introduced into the vagina, the false menses are weak; if it goes through the cotton without soaking through a piece of fabric put over the vagina, the false menses are medium; but if the blood goes through both cotton and fabric, the false menses are severe.

*

If a woman has weak false menses, she must wash according to the established rules before starting to pray, change the cotton or wash it, and also wash her vagina if it has been sullied by the flowing blood.

*

What we call the menstrual period is in fact a period consisting of several days during the month, when blood is discharged from the vagina. This blood is usually dense, hot, dark, or bright red, and flows out with a stinging sensation.

*

Women who are descendants of the Prophet become menopausal after sixty. All other women reach the age of menopause after fifty.

*

Therefore, the blood discharge from the vagina of a girl under the age of nine or from the vagina of a woman over sixty is not menstrual blood, and must not be considered so.

*

A pregnant woman and a nursing one may have regular periods, just like any other woman.

*

It is required that during the first three days of the menses, the blood not be ceased from flowing. In this way, one can make sure that, if the bleeding comes to an end after two days, only to start again the next day, this blood discharge is not menstrual.

*

It is not necessary that the bleeding be continuous for three days; it is enough that there be some blood in the vagina.

*

In case a woman notices that her vagina has been bleeding for more than three days and less than ten days, and is not certain whether the bleeding has been caused by menstruation or by an abscess, she must somehow introduce a piece of cotton into the vagina, and then pull it back. If the blood on the cotton starts to flow down on the left side, it is menstrual blood, and if it flows down on the right side, it is caused by an abscess.

*

If a woman notices that her vagina is bleeding and does not know whether the blood flow has been caused by menstruation or by her hymen, she must introduce a piece of cotton into her vagina and leave it there for a while before pulling it out. If the blood has soiled only the margins of the cotton, it is the blood of the hymen. If the entire piece of cotton is sullied, the blood is menstrual.

*

If a woman notices blood flowing from her vagina for a period of time shorter than three days, then stopping and flowing again for three days in a row, it is the second discharge of blood which is that of the menses, even if the first flow resembled the usual menstrual blood more than the other.

*

During menstruation, it is recommendable that a man abstain from having intercourse with his wife, even if it does not involve complete penetration – that means, as deep as the circumcision ring – and even if it does not involve sperm release. It is also preferable that one restrain from sodomizing a woman while she is having her period.

*

If the number of days of the woman's period is divided by three, a husband who becomes sexually intimate with her during the first two days must pay the equivalent of 18 *nokhod* [approximately 3 grams, or 1/10 ounce] of gold to the poor; if he has intercourse with her on the third or fourth day, he must pay the equivalent of 9 *nokhod*; and if he becomes intimate with her during the last two days of her period, the man has to pay the equivalent of 4 ½ *nokhod.*

*

Sodomizing a woman who is having her period does not require such alms.

*

In case a man engages in coitus with his wife during all the three periods that have been described above, he must pay the equivalent of 3 ½ *nokhod* of gold. If the rate of gold has changed between the time of the intercourse and that of payment, it is the price in effect on the day of payment that must be paid to the poor, and not that in effect on the day of the coitus.

*

In case a man does not afford to pay the required amount of money to the poor, he must give whatever he can afford to a needy person. If he cannot afford anything, being himself too poor, then he must beg Allah to forgive him.

*

When the menstrual period is over, a man may disallow his wife, even if she has not made her ablutions yet. He may have intercourse with her, but it is recommended that he wait until she has completed her ablutions. Meanwhile, the woman is not permitted to do anything which is restricted to her during the menstrual period, such as attending a mosque or touching the holy Koran, until she has performed her ablutions.

19

On Marriage, Adultery And Conjugal Life

A woman may legally belong to a man in the following two ways: by permanent marriage, or by temporary marriage. In the former, there is no need to mention the duration of the marriage; in the latter, the duration must be clearly stated, for example, for an hour, a day, a month, a year, or more.

*

Marriage, whether permanent or temporary, must be sealed by a spiritual formula uttered either by the woman or by the man, or by one of their representatives.

*

As long as the man and the woman have not been wed on the basis of a religious contract, they are not allowed to look upon one another. To have the permission to do this, it is not sufficient to assume that the sealing formula has been uttered, but if their representative declares that it has been uttered, then that is enough to make the marriage legitimate.

*

If a woman gives authorization to a person to marry her to a man for a certain period of time, ten days for example, without mentioning the exact date, the man may seal the marriage according to his will; yet, if the woman has mentioned a precise day and hour, the marriage-sealing formula must be said at the specified time.

*

The legal marriage-sealing formula must be said in Arabic. In case one cannot speak Arabic correctly, one is allowed to say it in a different language.

*

A father or a paternal grandfather holds the right to marry off a child who is mentally sick or has not reached the age of puberty by formally representing his descendant. The child is not permitted to cancel such an arranged marriage after reaching the age of puberty or regaining his or her mental health unless the marriage may somehow harm the child.

*

A girl who has grown up, that means a girl who can operate a distinction between what may be good and what may be not good for her, and who wishes to get married, being a virgin, is allowed to wed a man only if her father or paternal grandfather has consented. The consent of her mother or brother is not needed.

*

If a father or paternal grandfather marries off a son or grandson who has not yet reached the age of puberty, the latter will bear all responsibility, once he has reached the pubertal age, for providing for his wife.

*

A marriage is declared void if a man finds out that his wife is suffering from one of these seven afflictions: mental illness; leprosy; eczema; blindness; paralysis with permanent consequences; malformation of the urinary and genital tracts, or conjoined genital tract and rectum; vaginal malformation which makes intercourse impracticable.

*

In case a wife discovers after marriage that her husband is afflicted with madness, that he has been castrated, that he is impotent, or that he has had the testicles excised, she may file for cancellation of marriage.

*

If a wife has her marriage cancelled because her husband is not able to have intercourse with her either vaginally or anally, he must compensate her with half of the dowry that has been stipulated in the marriage contract. If the husband or wife cancels the marriage for any of the above-mentioned reasons, the man does not have to pay any compensation to the woman in case they have had intimate relations together. If the two have had no sexual relations, then the man must pay her the full amount of the dowry.

*

One is not permitted to marry his own mother, sister, or stepmother.

*

One is restricted from marrying his mother-in-law, his wife's maternal or paternal grandmothers, or any of her great-grandmothers, even if the man has no sexual relations with her.

*

A man who marries a woman and has sexual intercourse with her is not permitted to marry her daughters or granddaughters, even if they have resulted from another marriage.

*

One is not permitted to marry his wife's daughter, even if he does not have intimate relations with her.

*

The aunts of the bride's father and the aunts of the grandparents are not required to wear the veil in the presence of the groom. The father, grandfather, and great-grandfather of the groom, as well as his sons, grandsons, and all his male progeny are allowed to see the bride without the veil on.

*

A man is restricted to marry his wife's nieces unless he has his wife's consent. In case he, nevertheless, marries one of the nieces, but his wife fully agrees, then there is no interdiction.

*

A man who has been adulterous with his aunt is not allowed to marry her daughters, that means his first cousins.

*

In case a man who is married to his first cousin becomes adulterous with her mother, the marriage should not be terminated.

*

If a man becomes adulterous with a woman other than his aunt, it is advisable that he not marry the daughter of that woman. In case one marries a woman, has sexual intercourse with her, and then commits adultery with his wife's mother, it is not required that the marriage be terminated. Nor must it necessarily be cancelled if he becomes adulterous with his wife's mother before he has sexual relations with his wife, although it is recommended that the man annul the marriage himself.

*

An Islamic woman is not permitted to marry a non-Islamic man. An Islamic man is restricted from taking a non-Islamic woman in permanent marriage, but he is allowed to take a Jewish or Christian woman in temporary marriage.

*

A man who marries a woman who is already married must break off his marriage at once, and must never marry her again.

*

A married woman who has committed adultery with a man remains, from a legal perspective, still married. Nevertheless, if she does not repent and continues to sin by being unfaithful to her husband, the latter must repudiate her, but only after he has paid her dowry in full.

*

The mother, sister, or daughter of a man who has been sodomized by another man is permitted to refuse marrying the latter, even if both men, or at least one of them, had not yet reached the age of puberty at the time of the incident. However, if the victim is unable to prove it, his mother, sister, or daughter may marry the other man.

*

If a man who has married a girl under the age of puberty inflicts traumatisms upon her as a result of having sexual intercourse with her before the age of nine, he must refrain from possessing her sexually again.

*

If a man sodomizes his wife's son, brother, or father after he has married her, the marriage is not annulled.

*

A woman who is engaged in a permanent marriage is not entitled to go out of the house without her husband's consent. She must be at all times at his disposal for the gratification of any of his desires; she is not allowed to refuse herself to him except for a pertinent reason, such as a religious one. If she fully submits to him, the husband has the obligation to provide food, clothing, and housing for her, regardless of whether he has the means to do so or not.

*

A woman who refuses herself to her husband makes herself guilty of rejection, and should not expect him to provide food, clothing, housing, or any later sexual intimacy. Yet, she is still entitled to the prescribed compensation in case the husband repudiates her.

*

In case a wife wishes to undertake a travel, the husband is not required to pay for it if the travel exceeds the regular expenses incurred by his wife at home. Nevertheless, if he sends her somewhere, then he must meet all the travel expenses.

*

A wife who fully submits to her husband has the right to be paid the daily household expenses for any of the husband's properties if he is not willing to pay for them. However, if she is compelled to pay these expenses with her own money, then she may disobey her husband.

*

A man who is engaged in a permanent marriage is restricted from leaving his wife for so long a period of time as to make her wonder whether the marriage is still valid or not. Still, he is not required to accept her company one night out of every four.

*

A husband has the duty to please his wife at least once in every four months.

*

If, at the time of sealing the marriage, no mention was made in regard to the time at which the husband was supposed to pay the dowry to his wife, the wife is permitted to refuse herself to her husband for as long as the conditions of the marriage concerning the dowry have not been fulfilled. However, once she has consented to have sexual intercourse with her husband, she is not allowed to later refuse herself to him, except for religious reasons.

*

A temporary marriage, be it one of convenience only, is legal from all perspectives.

*

One must not abstain from having sexual intimacy with his temporary wife for more than four months.

*

If the temporary marriage contract comprises a clause

mentioning that the husband does not have the right to have normal sexual relations with his wife, such a regulation must be at all times obeyed. In this case, he must restrict himself to pleasure her otherwise. However, as soon as the temporary wife agrees to have normal sexual relations with her husband, he is allowed to have normal intercourse with her.

*

A woman who has contracted a temporary marriage in exchange for a certain dowry is not entitled to supplementary funds for covering her daily expenses, even if she is pregnant.

*

A temporary wife is not entitled to any inheritance from her husband; nor is the husband entitled to any inheritance from her.

*

A woman engaged in a temporary marriage has the right to go out of the house without asking her husband's permission, unless her going out might somehow harm him.

*

If a father (or paternal grandfather) marries off his daughter (or granddaughter) in her absence without proof that she is alive, the marriage is terminated once it has been proven that she was deceased at the time the marriage was contracted.

*

A man must not look upon the body of a woman other than his wife under any circumstance. A woman must also not look upon the body of a man other than her husband under any pretext whatsoever.

*

Looking upon the face and hair of a prepubic girl is generally allowed, provided that one looks upon her without lust and without fear of temptation. Nevertheless, it is advisable that one not look upon the girl's belly and thighs, which must be covered at all times.

*

Looking upon the face and hands of a Jewish or Christian woman is most of the time allowed, but only as long as the man does not fear that he will somehow succumb to the temptation of sexual gratification.

*

A woman must hide her body and hair from the eyes of men. It is advisable that she also hide her body and hair from the boys who have not reached puberty, in case she fears that they might look upon her with lustful eyes.

*

One must not look upon the genitals of another person, even from behind a glass, or in a mirror, or in still waters. It is highly recommended that one refrain from looking at the genitals of a child who is able to tell the difference between good and evil. However, a husband and a wife may look upon each other in all parts of their bodies.

*

It is forbidden for a man to look upon the body of another man with lusty eyes. Similarly, a woman must not look upon another woman with lust.

*

A man is permitted to photograph a woman who is not his wife, provided that he does not have to touch her in order to take her picture.

*

In case a woman has to give an enema to a woman or to a man other than her husband, or to wash their genital organs, then she is required to cover her hand in order to avoid direct contact with the genitals. The same applies to a man where another man or a woman other than his wife is involved.

*

If a man has to look upon a woman other than his wife and touch her body for medical reasons, then he is allowed to do so. Nevertheless, if he can administer medical care by just looking at her body, then he must not touch it, and if he cannot diagnose her without touching her body, then he must not look at it.

*

If a man or woman is required to look upon the genitals of another person for medical reasons, then he or she must do so in an indirect manner, namely by looking in a mirror, except in a situation when looking at a person's genitals becomes a stringent necessity.

*

In case the husband has inserted into the marriage contract a clause stipulating the guarantee of his future wife's virginity, then he is permitted to cancel the marriage if it turns out that she was not a virgin at the time the marriage was sealed.

*

If a woman commits apostasy before her marriage is consummated, the marriage is terminated; this is also true after completion of the marriage, if the woman is menopausal. However, if she is not menopausal and returns to the Islamic fold within a hundred days after the annulment of the marriage, it becomes valid again.

*

A man whose father or mother was an Islamist at the time he was conceived, and who became an Islamist himself at the age of puberty, will have his marriage automatically annulled if he abjures his own faith.

*

The marriage of a man born of non-Islamic parents, but who have converted to Islam, is automatically abolished if he becomes an apostate before consummating the marriage. If he abjures his faith after he has had sexual intercourse with his wife, she must wait exactly a hundred days before getting married again, if she is old enough to have menstrual periods. In this case, the marriage maintains its validity, if during the one hundred days the husband returns to his Islamic beliefs; in all other instances, the marriage termination cannot be revoked.

*

If the woman includes in the marriage contract a clause stipulating that her husband is not supposed to move her away from the city, and the husband agrees with it, then he must respect this clause.

*

The husband of a woman who has had a daughter by a previous marriage has the right to marry that girl to a son he has had by a previous marriage. He is also entitled to marry the mother of a girl who has married his son.

*

A woman who becomes pregnant as a consequence of having committed adultery must not abort her child.

*

If a man becomes adulterous with an unmarried woman, and subsequently marries her, the child born of that union is to be considered a bastard, unless the parents are certain that the baby was conceived after they had gotten married.

*

A man must not believe a woman who asserts that she has become menopausal. Nevertheless, he must believe her in case she tells him that she is not married.

*

It is advisable that a girl be married off as soon as she reaches puberty. One of greatest blessings bestowed upon a man is to have his daughter experience her first menstrual period, not in her father's house, but in that of her husband.

*

A child born of a father who has committed adultery is to be considered legitimate.

*

Having sexual intercourse with one's wife during the fast of Ramadan or while she is having her period is a transgression; however, the child born of such a sinful relation must be considered legitimate.

*

If a man marries a woman and has sexual relations with her, he is restricted from marrying any of the girls whom his wife has breast-fed.

*

A man is not permitted to marry a wet nurse who has breast-fed his own wife.

*

A man is not allowed to marry a girl who was breast-fed, when a baby, by his mother or grandmother.

*

It is highly recommended that a newborn baby be breast-fed by the mother. Normally, she is not supposed to be paid for this, but her husband may pay her for rendering this service if he considers it appropriate. If the price asked by the mother is higher than that usually charged by a wet nurse, the husband may hire a wet nurse for breast-feeding his child.

*

It is advisable that the wet nurse be a devout Shi'ite, smart, humble, and pretty. On the other side, it is forbidden to hire a retarded wet nurse, or one who repudiates the Twelve Imams, who is ugly, a bastard, or unreliable. One is also restricted from hiring as wet nurse a woman who has an illegitimate child.

*

It is preferable that a child be breast-fed for a period of exactly two years.

20

On Divorce

A man who repudiates his wife must have a healthy mind and must have passed the age of puberty. The repudiation must not be dictated or enforced by anybody else. Thus, if the divorce decree is pronounced as a joke, the marriage is not terminated.

*

At the time of the divorce, the woman must not be having her menstrual period, and the man must not have been intimate with her since her last menstruation.

*

However, a husband is permitted to repudiate his wife while she is having her menstrual period under three circumstances: if he has had no sexual intercourse with her since they were married; if she is pregnant while the husband believes that she is having her menstrual period, and it is discovered only later that she was with child at the time she was repudiated; if the husband does not know that his wife is having her menstrual period because they are separated by a distance.

*

A man who has had intercourse with his wife after her last period will have to postpone the divorce until she has the next menstrual period. Nevertheless, he is allowed to divorce his wife if she has not turned nine yet, or if she is pregnant, or if she has reached menopause.

*

In case a man who has been intimate with his wife between two menstrual periods divorces her while she is having her period and finds out only later that she was with child when the divorce formula was pronounced, the divorce is to be considered legitimate.

*

A temporarily married woman, be it for a month or a year, has her marriage automatically terminated at the end of the marital contract, or at any other time when her temporary husband discharges her from her contractual obligations. No witnesses are required, and there is no need that the woman be past her menstrual period.

*

A woman who has not yet had her ninth birthday or a woman who has entered menopause is allowed to get remarried right after a divorce, without having to wait for a hundred days, as it is otherwise required.

*

A woman who has already turned nine, or who is not yet menopausal, must wait for three menstrual periods after she has divorced her husband before she may get remarried.

*

If a woman who has not yet reached the age of nine or who has not yet turned menopausal contracts a temporary marriage, she is obliged, when the marriage ends, or whenever her temporary husband has discharged her from contractual obligations, wait two menstrual periods or exactly forty-five days before being allowed to remarry.

*

In case a man becomes adulterous with a woman other than his wife, and he is aware that she is not his wife, while the woman has no knowledge that the man is not her husband, she must wait for a period of one hundred days before marrying again.

*

If a man pursues a legally married woman to leave her husband in order to marry him, they are both guilty of a terrible sin; however, the divorce and the new marriage remain valid.

*

If the father or paternal grandfather of a boy arranges for him a temporary marriage, he is permitted to annul it earlier than established provided that the cancellation is for the boy's benefit, even if the marriage was sealed before the boy reached puberty. For instance, if a fourteen-year-old boy has been married off to a woman for a period of two years, they may release her from the balance of her contractual engagement.

Nevertheless, a permanent marriage cannot be broken in this way.

*

In case a husband repudiates his wife without informing her about his decision, and does not stop paying her expenses for a period of, let us say, one year, and at the end of that interval he lets her know that he divorced her a year earlier and brings forth proof of it, he may ask her to return to him anything that he has bought or given her as a gift during that period, on condition that she has not spent it or exhausted it, in which case she is not required to return it anymore.

21

On Funerary Rites

If a limb or any other part is separated from the body, whether before or after death, and if one touches it when the ablution of the corpse has not yet been performed, then one must subject oneself to a cleansing ritual. However, if the detached part does not contain any bone, the cleansing is not required.

*

If one touches the bone or tooth of a dead body, cleansing is needed; yet, ablution is not necessary if the bone or tooth belongs to a living body, unless there is some muscle attached to it. One must by all means refrain from leaving a dying person alone, placing something heavy on his belly, leaving him in the care of a man who has recently ejaculated or a woman who is having her menstrual period, talking too much around him, crying, or leaving him in the care of women only.

*

The cleansing of a deceased man by a woman is prohibited, and so is the cleansing of a deceased woman by a man. Yet, the woman may perform the ablution if the dead man is her husband, and vice-versa. Nevertheless, it is preferable that they refrain from it.

*

It is strictly prohibited to look upon the genitalia of a deceased man or woman. The persons performing the cleansing ritual commit an unpardonable transgression if they disobey this restriction; however, in such a case the cleansing remains valid.

*

During the ablution, the sexual organs of the corpse must be covered at all times, even if only by a piece of wood or by a brick.

*

In case one dies by drowning in a well, and consequently it is impossible to get the corpse out, the well must be sealed and turned into his tomb.

*

If a baby dies in its mother's womb and leaving it there might threaten the mother's life, then the child must be pulled out in the most simple way, no matter how, even by being cut into pieces, if needed. The job must be done either by the woman's husband or by a hired woman.

*

No one has the right to exhume the body of an Islamist, not even that of a child or that of a mad person, if it has not yet turned to dust.

*

One is permitted to exhume a body provided that it is done for taking out of it a child presumed to be still alive in its mother's womb, or if one reckons that the body might be subjected to a wild beast's feast, or because a torrent might carry it away, or because it might fall into the hands of the enemy. One is also allowed to reopen a tomb for placing in it a part of one's dead body, in case it has been found or recuperated after the corpse has been buried.

22

On Finance and Taxes

Any commercial transaction which involves one or more of the following transgressions is to be considered illegitimate, and consequently it must be forbidden: trade in urine, excrement, alcohol, illicit riches (unless the buyer thereof agrees to the terms of the transaction), musical instruments, gambling paraphernalia, merchandise commercialized with an interest on a loan offered for the purchase, adulterated products (unless the buyer is informed of it, prior to the closing of the transaction).

*

Trade in oil, medicine, and perfumes imported from non-Islamic countries is permitted, on condition that their uncleanness has not been proven. On the other side, one must know that fat is unclean if it is produced in an Islamic country and comes from an animal which is unknown to have been slaughtered according to the Islamic law. Trade in such products is illicit.

*

It is forbidden to trade skins of foxes which died or were slaughtered in a way that contravenes the Islamic regulations.

*

Trade in meat, fat, and skins is allowed on condition that the merchant is an Islamist. However, it is strictly forbidden if the purchaser knows that this Islamist has acquired the products from an infidel, unless it is clearly proved that the animals were slaughtered according to the well-established Islamic precepts.

*

Any trade in objects used for entertainment, such as musical instruments, regardless of their size, is by all means illicit.

*

An Islamist is permitted to require from an infidel payment of interest on a sum of money that he has lent him. This is also permitted between father and child, and between husband and wife.

*

Those who work in oil deposits, or gold, silver, lead, copper, iron, turquoise, salt or other mines must pay the *khoms* [tax in the amount of one-fifth of one's income] to the Islamic Treasury if the profit made by him from such activities reaches the required minimum, namely the value of coins consisting of 415 grams of silver or 45 grams of gold, after all the expenses have been deducted. If the profit made is lower than the above-mentioned figures, the *khoms* must still be paid if the gross income of this person exceeds annual expenses.

*

If one discovers a treasure whose value is at least that of coins of 415 grams of silver or 45 grams of gold, the *khoms* is still due.

*

If a person purchases an animal and after its killing discovers in its belly a precious object, he must ask the seller if the object is his. If the valuable object does not belong to him, he must inquire of the previous owners. If the buyer learns that that the object belongs to none of them, then he must pay the *khoms* to the Islamic Treasury, even if the value of the object is lower than that of 145 grams of silver or 45 grams of gold.

*

In case one dives into a river known to contain jewels, such as the Tigris or the Euphrates, and comes up with such a jewel, this person must pay the *khoms* according to its true value.

*

If a person dives into a river and comes up with a quantity of amber whose value exceeds that of 4 grams of gold, he must pay the *khoms*, even if the respective quantity of amber was collected through more than one dive.

*

If a child discovers a mine or a treasure, or finds a jewel in a river, his father or legal guardian must pay the *khoms* according to its value.

*

The income from the *khoms* collected throughout the country must be divided between the *seyed* [the Prophet's descendents] and the Holy Imam, whose representative in our age is a *modjtahed* [learned man]. The *seyed*'s share is to be apportioned, with the *modjtahed*'s blessing, to the *seyed* who are destitute, orphaned, or ruined. The Imam's share is to be spent only with the permission of His sole representative on earth, namely the *modjtahed*.

*

The *zakat* [tithe] for camels must be calculated on the ground of twelve brackets:

-one sheep for five camels;
-two sheep for five camels;
-three sheep for fifteen camels;
-four sheep for twenty camels;
-five sheep for twenty-five camels;
-one second-year camel for twenty-six camels;
-one third-year camel for thirty-six camels;
-one fourth-year camel for forty-six camels;
-one fifth-year camel for sixty-one camels;
-two third-year camels for seventy-six camels;
-two-fourth year camels for ninety-one camels;
-for 120 camels or more, one must count one three-year-old camel for every forty camels, or calculate by brackets for fifty and forty, making sure that no one has been overlooked. Yet, if

there are any left over, the remainder must not be more than nine. For instance, if one owns 140 camels, he must give as *zakat* two four-year-old camels for the first hundred, and one three-year-old camel for the remaining forty. All camels given as *zakat* must be females.

Addenda

It is highly recommended that a man refrain from shaving his face, whether with a bladed razor or with an electric one.

*

The use of drums during sports competitions is not permitted; nor is the playing of military marches during military parades, if such music can be associated in any way with lubricous music.

*

Gambling is strictly prohibited, even if it is only for entertainment, and not for monetary gain.

*

No Islamist is allowed to work for a Jewish company, if he knows, or somehow suspects, that this company offers support for Israel. The money paid by such a company is unclean.

*

It is not really forbidden for Islamists to work for a firm run by an Islamist who also employs Jews, as long as the company does not serve Israel in any way whatsoever. Yet, it is humiliating to work under the orders of a Jewish supervisor.

*

It is strictly prohibited to dissect the dead body of an Islamist; however, the dissection of non-Islamic corpses is allowed.

*

The flesh of an animal slaughtered by a machine, as those recently employed by slaughterers in various countries, is unclean, and is forbidden either to sell or to buy it. In the transaction of such impure meat, the seller owes the buyer the money he has paid for it, even if the animal was slaughtered by an Islamist facing the *Qibla* [the direction of Mecca], and even if Allah was invoked at the time of the slaughtering.

*

Meat imported from the infidels' countries is always unclean, and must be considered identical with the flesh of a human body, unless it is clearly proven that the animals were slaughtered according to the well-established Islamic principles.

*

It is strictly forbidden to look upon a woman other than one's wife, or an animal, or a statue, in a lustful or licentious way.

*

A woman who wants to have a better education in order to pursue a respectable career, and who has a male teacher, may continue her studies only if she covers her face and has no physical contact with men. However, if contact with men is inevitable, or if religious and moral precepts are in any manner whatsoever neglected, then she must give up her studies.

*

Young males and females who attend mixed classes in elementary schools, high schools, universities, or other educational institutions, and who, in order to make such studies legal, wish to seal such a temporary marriage, are permitted to do so without their fathers' authorization. The same rule applies if a boy and a girl are in love with each other, but hesitate to ask for their fathers' permission.

www.ingramcontent.com/pod-product-compliance
Ingram Content Group UK Ltd.
Pitfield, Milton Keynes, MK11 3LW, UK
UKHW020222250726
13967UKWH00001B/148